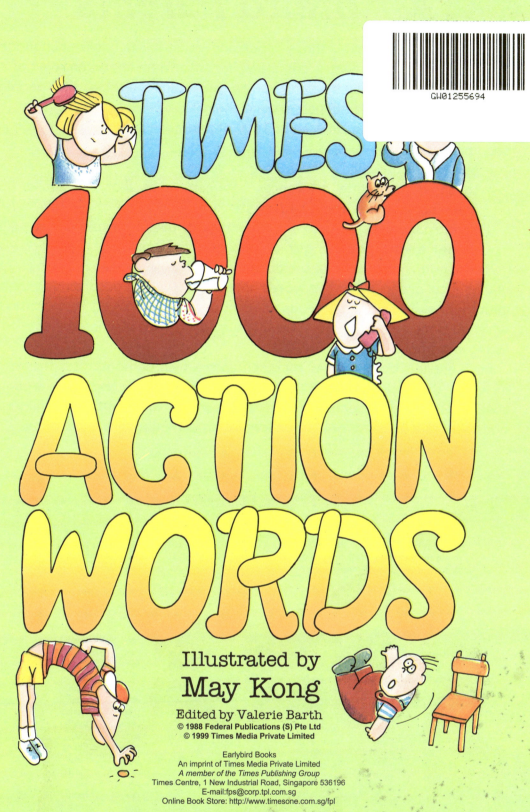

Times 1000 ACTION WORDS

Illustrated by **May Kong**

Edited by Valerie Barth

© 1988 Federal Publications (S) Pte Ltd
© 1999 Times Media Private Limited

Earlybird Books
An imprint of Times Media Private Limited
A member of the Times Publishing Group
Times Centre, 1 New Industrial Road, Singapore 536196
E-mail:fps@corp.tpl.com.sg
Online Book Store: http://www.timesone.com.sg/fpl

First published 1988
Reprinted 1989, 1990 (three times), 1992 (three times), 1993 (twice), 1994, 1995, 1996, 1997 (twice), 1999, 2000

All rights reserved. No part of this publication may be reproduced, stored in a retrieval system, or transmitted, in any form or by any means, electronic, mechanical, photocopying, recording or otherwise, without the prior permission of the publishers.
ISBN 981 01 0383 2
Printed by JBW Printers & Binders Pte Ltd, Singapore

earlybird books

A Note to Parents

Action words are verbs — those important words in the English Language without which no sentence is complete. Verbs form an important part of a child's vocabulary. They help children to talk about the things that people do and the things that happen around them.

This book introduces children to 1000 of the more common verbs. It has been prepared with three principal aims in mind:

- to enlarge the child's vocabulary of verbs;
- to show the subtle differences between verbs that are similar in meaning, e.g. **see**, **look**, **glare**, **stare**;
- to introduce the child to the meanings of useful phrasal verbs such as **get away**, **get off**, **get on** and **get up**.

Please note, however, that the action words have not been listed in strict alphabetical order. While the words have been grouped according to their initial letters, within each group they have been arranged in a context which is more logical or more visually appealing than a strict alphabetical listing would allow.

Each entry is accompanied by a sentence which demonstrates the way in which the action word is typically used in the context of everyday speech. The lively and amusing illustrations will certainly appeal to children and make the learning of new action words an enjoyable experience.

Pronunciation Key

Vowels

i:	as in	bead	[bi:d]
ɪ	as in	bid	[bɪd]

Vowels represented by i (e.g. baby ['beɪbi], pedestrian [pə'dɛstrɪən]) can be pronounced as i: or ɪ.

ɛ	as in	bed	[bɛd]
æ	as in	bad	[bæd]
ɑ:	as in	card	[kɑ:d]
ʌ	as in	bud	[bʌd]
ɒ	as in	body	['bɒdi]
ɔ:	as in	board	[bɔ:d]
ʊ	as in	good	[gʊd]
u:	as in	food	[fu:d]

Vowels represented by u (e.g. occupy ['ɒkjupaɪ], vacuum ['vækjuəm]) can be pronounced as u: or ʊ.

ɜ:	as in	bird	[bɜ:d]
ə	as in	cupboard	['kʌbəd]
eɪ	as in	paid	[peɪd]
aɪ	as in	died	[daɪd]
ɔɪ	as in	avoid	[ə'vɔɪd]
aʊ	as in	loud	[laʊd]
əʊ	as in	load	[ləʊd]
ɪə	as in	beard	[bɪəd]
ɛə	as in	cared	[kɛəd]
ʊə	as in	cured	[kjʊəd]

Consonants

p	as in	pin	[pɪn]
		rip	[rɪp]
b	as in	bin	[bɪn]
		rib	[rɪb]
t	as in	tin	[tɪn]
		written	['rɪtn]
d	as in	din	[dɪn]
		rid	[rɪd]
k	as in	cane	[keɪn]
		Rick	[rɪk]
g	as in	gain	[geɪn]
		rig	[rɪg]
tʃ	as in	chin	[tʃɪn]
		rich	[rɪtʃ]
dʒ	as in	gin	[dʒɪn]
		ridge	[rɪdʒ]
m	as in	met	[mɛt]
		ram	[ræm]
n	as in	net	[nɛt]
		ran	[ræn]
ŋ	as in	rang	[ræŋ]
f	as in	fine	[faɪn]
		life	[laɪf]
v	as in	vine	[vaɪn]
		alive	[ə'laɪv]
θ	as in	thin	[θɪn]
		breath	[brɛθ]
ð	as in	this	[ðɪs]
		breathe	[bri:ð]
s	as in	sin	[sɪn]
		rice	[raɪs]
z	as in	zoo	[zu:]
		rise	[raɪz]
ʃ	as in	shin	[ʃɪn]
		wish	[wɪʃ]
ʒ	as in	measure	['mɛʒə]
		vision	['vɪʒn]
h	as in	head	[hɛd]
l	as in	let	[lɛt]
		tell	[tɛl]
r	as in	red	[rɛd]
w	as in	wet	[wɛt]
j	as in	yet	[jɛt]

The mark ' shows that the following syllable is stressed, e.g. finish ['fɪnɪʃ], arrive [ə'raɪv].

Aa

answer ['ɑːnsə]
Helen is **answering** the telephone.

accept [ək'sɛpt]
Kathy **accepts** a gift from her father.

add [æd]
Mother is **adding** some milk to her coffee.

attend [ə'tɛnd]
We are **attending** Jane's birthday party.

add up ['æd 'ʌp]
Teacher asked me to **add up** these numbers.

act [ækt]
Jimmy **acted** as a wolf in the school play.

awake [ə'weɪk]
The alarm clock **awoke** me from sleep.

admire [əd'maɪə]
Jane's friends **admire** her beautiful new doll.

1

Bb

bleed [bli:d]
Jimmy's arm is **bleeding**.

bandage ['bændɪdʒ]
The nurse is **bandaging** Jimmy's arm.

bake [beɪk]
Mother is **baking** a cake for Kathy's birthday.

belong [bɪ'lɒŋ]
This book **belongs** to me. It is mine.

barbecue ['bɑ:bɪkju:]
Father is **barbecuing** in the backyard.

bark [bɑ:k]
The dogs are **barking** loudly at the cat.

bath [bɑ:θ]
Mother **baths** the baby in warm water.

beat [bi:t]
Mandy is **beating** an egg.

Jimmy is **beating** the drum.

Helen **beats** Willy in the race.

break [breɪk]
Willy **broke** the stick into two pieces.

break down [ˈbreɪk ˈdaʊn]
Father's car **broke down** on his way to work.

blush [blʌʃ]
Linda **blushed** when Jimmy gave her a kiss.

bend [bɛnd]
Willy is **bending** a stick.

Benny **bends** down to pick a coin.

block [blɒk]
The fallen tree is **blocking** the road.

box [bɒks]
That big boy **boxed** Andy on the chin.

bounce [baʊns]
Andy is **bouncing** a ball.

bow [baʊ]
The magician is **bowing** to the audience.

button [ˈbʌtn]
Helen is **buttoning** up her jacket.

beg [bɛg]
The clever dog **begs** for a bone.

bring [brɪŋ]
Mother is **bringing** us some food.

boil [bɔɪl]
The water is **boiling**.
Mother will switch the kettle off.

borrow [ˈbɒrəʊ]
Helen is **borrowing** books from the library.

balance [ˈbæləns]
Andy is **balancing** a ball on his forehead.

Uncle Roy is **blowing** his nose.
He has a cold.

blow [bləʊ]
The wind is **blowing** through the trees.

bite [baɪt]
The dog is **biting** a bone.

blow up [ˈbləʊ ˈʌp]
Andy is **blowing up** a balloon.

blow out [ˈbləʊ ˈaʊt]
Jane **blows out** the candles on her birthday cake.

bury ['bɛri']
The dog is **burying** a bone.

burn [bɜːn]
Father is **burning** some leaves.

brush [brʌʃ]
Jimmy is **brushing** his teeth.
Kathy is **brushing** her hair.

breathe [briːð]
We **breathe** through our noses.

burst [bɜːst]
The balloon **burst** with a loud bang.

bump [bʌmp]
Willy **bumped** into a street lamp.

build [bɪld]
Peter is **building** a spaceship.

buy [baɪ]
Mandy is **buying** some flowers.

bully ['bʊli]
That big boy is **bullying** the little children.

Cc

camp [kæmp]
The scouts **camped** at the beach.

call [kɔːl]
Call the firemen to put out the fire.

call for [ˈkɔːl fə]
Willy **called for** help when he got into trouble while swimming.

call off [ˈkɔːl ˈɒf]
The teacher had to **call off** the picnic because it was raining.

catch [kætʃ]
Jimmy held out both hands to **catch** the ball.

change [tʃeɪndʒ]
Willy **changed** out of his wet clothes into dry ones.

care [kɛə]
Simon **cares** for his pet rabbit. He feeds it and cleans its cage every day.

catch up [ˈkætʃ ˈʌp]
The snail cannot **catch up** with the rabbit. He is too slow.

cause [kɔːz]
Willy's sneeze **caused** the glass of water to fall over.

8

carry ['kæri]
Mother is **carrying** the baby.

carry on ['kæri 'ɒn]
Grandmother let me **carry on** watching television although it was past my bedtime.

celebrate ['sɛləbreɪt]
Jane is **celebrating** her birthday by having a party.

chat [tʃæt]
Kathy is **chatting** with her friends.

cheat [tʃi:t]
Jimmy **cheated** at cards.

choose [tʃu:z]
It is hard to **choose** which sweets to buy when they all look so nice.

chip [tʃɪp]
Andy dropped a plate and **chipped** it.

$7 + 8 = ?$
(a) 5 (b) 10 (c) 15

chase [tʃeɪs]
The dog **chased** the cat up a tree.

carve [kɑ:v]
Peter is **carving** a piece of wood into a boat.

circle ['sɜ:kl]
Helen is **circling** the right answer to the sum.

9

check [tʃɛk]

Linda is counting her school books to **check** if she has them all.

check in [ˈtʃɛk ˈɪn]

We **checked in** to the hotel at the start of our holiday.

check out [ˈtʃɛk ˈaʊt]

We were sad to **check out** of the hotel at the end of our holiday.

cling [klɪŋ]

The baby koala **clings** tightly to its mother.

check up [ˈtʃɛk ˈʌp]

We are going to see a movie tonight. Simon is **checking up** on the times of the shows.

chop [tʃɒp]

Uncle Roy **chopped** down the tree.

charge [tʃɑːdʒ]

The rhinoceros **charged** at the fence.

cheer [tʃɪə]

The girls are **cheering** their team at the race.

cheer up [ˈtʃɪər ˈʌp]

The cartoon show **cheered up** the children and made them laugh.

clap [klæp]

When the show ended, the children **clapped** their hand

clean [kli:n]
Father **cleans** the car on Sundays.

clean up [ˈkli:n ˈʌp]
Mother told Jimmy to **clean up** his room.

chew [tʃu:]
The dog is **chewing** a bone.

clear [klɪə]
I am **clearing** the desk so that I have room to do my homework.

clear away [ˈklɪər əˈweɪ]
Kathy helps father **clear away** the dishes after dinner.

clear up [ˈklɪər ˈʌp]
The children are **clearing up** the mess after the funfair.

clear off [ˈklɪər ˈɒf]
The thief **cleared off** when he saw a policeman coming.

clear out [ˈklɪər ˈaʊt]
Dad is **clearing out** the garage.

climb [klaɪm]
The baby **climbed** up a chair.

cluck [klʌk]
A hen **clucks** loudly after it has laid an egg.

clip [klɪp]

Mandy is **clipping** the papers together so that they will not get lost.

collect [kə'lɛkt]

Peter **collects** stamps from around the world.

complain [kəm'pleɪn]

Kathy **complained** to mother that Andy had torn her book.

coach [kəutʃ]

Mr Thomson **coaches** the soccer team.
He shows them how to kick the ball.

colour ['kʌlə]

Andy is **colouring** a picture of a lion.

comb [kəum]

Jane is **combing** her long hair.

close [kləuz]

Mother is **closing** the door.

congratulate [kən'grætʃuleɪt]

Everyone **congratulated** the winner.

coil [kɔɪl]

Father **coiled** the garden hose after he had watered the plants.

collapse [kə'læps]

The tent **collapsed** in the strong wind.

confuse [kən'fju:z]
The signs **confused** the driver.

collide [kə'laɪd]
The car **collided** with a van.

come [kʌm]
Come with me.
I'll show you the way.

come off ['kʌm 'ɒf]
A button **came off** Kathy's coat.

compare [kəm'pɛə]
Benny is tall **compared** with Helen.

come apart ['kʌm ə'pɑ:t]
The shirt was too small and **came apart** at the seam when Willy put it on.

come out ['kʌm 'aʊt]
The moon and star **come out** at night.

come across ['kʌm ə'krɒs]
Andy **came across** a gold chain while looking for his lost marble.

come back ['kʌm 'bæk]
Boomerangs always **come back** when thrown.

come on ['kʌm 'ɒn]
The magician **came on** the stage wearing a long black cape.

connect [kə'nɛkt]

Uncle Roy **connected** the aerial to the television.

consider [kən'sɪdə]

Mother and father are **considering** what to get for Kathy for her birthday.

consist [kən'sɪst]

This gift set **consists** of two storybooks and two tapes.

construct [kən'strʌkt]

Peter **constructed** a spaceship from clothes pegs.

continue [kən'tɪnju:]

"Mother, don't stop now. Please **continue** reading the story," the children asked.

control [kən'trəʊl]

Andy **controls** the robot by remote control.

cool [ku:l]

Mandy is **cooling** her feet in the stream.

cool off ['ku:l 'ɒf]

The children felt hot, so they jumped into the water to **cool off**.

cool down ['ku:l 'daʊn]

The porridge was hot, so the three bears left it to **cool down**.

contain [kən'teɪn]
This bottle **contains** ink.

cover ['kʌvə]
Kathy **covered** her face with her hands.

cover up ['kʌvər 'ʌp]
Andy **covered up** the ink stain so his mother would not see it.

copy ['kɒpi]
Linda **copied** the sums from the blackboard.

contribute [kən'trɪbju:t]
The children **contributed** some money to buy a present for their mother.

cook [kʊk]
Mother **cooked** a delicious roast chicken.

cost [kɒst]
This hamburger **costs** $1.30.

count [kaʊnt]
The rich man is **counting** his money.

cough [kɒf]
Willy **coughed** because he had a sore throat.

crack [kræk]
The vase **cracked** when it was dropped.

crash [kræʃ]
The car **crashed** into the wall.

create [kri'eɪt]
The magician **created** a monster with his spells.

crawl [krɔ:l]
The baby is **crawling** across the room.

crouch [kraʊtʃ]
Kathy **crouched** behind a chair to hide from Willy.

creep [kri:p]
Jimmy **crept** up behind Linda to frighten her.

cross [krɒs]
We looked left and right before **crossing** the street.

croak [krəʊk]
The frogs are **croaking** a song.

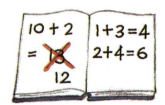

cry [kraɪ]
Jane **cried** when she fell down and hurt her knee.

cross out ['krɒs 'aʊt]
Peter **crossed out** a mistake in his book.

crumple [ˈkrʌmpl]

Andy **crumpled** up the drawing.

cuddle [ˈkʌdl]

The baby is **cuddling** a teddy bear.

crumble [ˈkrʌmbl]

Mother is **crumbling** the biscuit into a bowl.

cycle [ˈsaɪkl]

Bobby **cycles** home from school.

crow [krəʊ]

The rooster **crows** loudly in the early morning.

crush [krʌʃ]

The soccer ball was **crushed** by the steam roller.

curtsy [ˈkɜ:tsi]

Cinderella **curtsied** to the queen.

curl [kɜ:l]

The cat **curled** up on the cushion.

crowd [kraʊd]

The children are **crowding** around the friendly chimpanzee.

cut [kʌt]
Aunt Molly is **cutting** the cake into slices.

cut down ['kʌt 'daʊn]
Father **cut down** a tree in the garden.

cut off ['kʌt 'ɒf]
Bobby is **cutting off** the sleeves from his T-shirt.

cut out ['kʌt 'aʊt]
Linda is **cutting out** pictures from a magazine.

cut up ['kʌt 'ʌp]
Kathy **cuts up** the vegetables to make a salad.

Dd

damage ['dæmɪdʒ]
The ship was **damaged** when it hit the rocks.

dance [dɑ:ns]
The children are **dancing** happily round the Christmas tree.

dare [dɛə]
Andy didn't **dare** touch the snake.

darn [dɑ:n]
Mother is **darning** a hole in Jimmy's sock.

dash [dæʃ]

The dog **dashed** across the street.

describe [dɪ'skraɪb]

Jimmy is **describing** to the policeman the dog that he has lost.

demand [dɪ'mɑ:nd]

The spoilt child **demanded** the biggest ice-cream.

decorate ['dɛkəreɪt]

Mandy is **decorating** the hall.

delight [dɪ'laɪt]

Jane was **delighted** with her new puppy.

deliver [dɪ'lɪvə]

The postman **delivered** a parcel to Linda's house.

decide [dɪ'saɪd]

Helen could not **decide** whether to wear shorts or a dress.

deal [di:l]

You **deal** all the cards to play Snap.

deserve [dɪ'zɜ:v]

Bobby practised hard for the swimming contest and **deserved** first prize.

defend [dɪ'fɛnd]
The soldiers are **defending** their country from attack.

die [daɪ]
The bear **died** after the hunter shot it.

develop [dɪ'vɛləp]
The bodybuilder **developed** huge muscles.

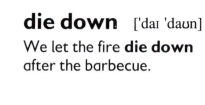

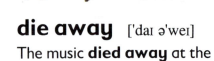

die down ['daɪ 'daʊn]
We let the fire **die down** after the barbecue.

die away ['daɪ ə'weɪ]
The music **died away** at the end of the song.

destroy [dɪ'strɔɪ]
The big boy **destroyed** Andy's sandcastle.

dig [dɪg]
Uncle Roy is **digging** a hole to plant the tree.

dial [daɪl]
Helen **dialed** 999 to call the police.

design [dɪ'zaɪn]
Aunt Molly is **designing** a party dress for Kathy.

demonstrate ['dɛmənstreɪt]
The fireman **demonstrated** how to put out the fire.

disguise
[dɪsˈgaɪz]

The thief **disguised** himself as an old lady.

direct [daɪˈrɛkt]

The policeman is **directing** the traffic at the crossroads.

dismiss
[dɪsˈmɪs]

At the end of the day the children are **dismissed** from class.

disappear
[dɪsəˈpɪə]

The wizard **disappeared** in a puff of smoke.

display
[dɪˈspleɪ]

The new books are **displayed** in the shop window.

dip [dɪp]

The cat **dipped** its paw into the fish tank to try to catch a fish.

discover
[dɪˈskʌvə]

The scientist **discovered** a new plant in the forest.

disturb
[dɪˈstɜːb]

Do not **disturb** Dad. He is sleeping.

discuss
[dɪˈskʌs]

Willy, Linda and Jimmy **discussed** where they wanted to go for a picnic.

do [duː]

Jimmy must **do** his homework. He cannot play with Andy now.

dream [ˈdriːm]

Helen **dreams** of being a pilot.

dock [dɒk]

The ship **docked** at the wharf to unload its cargo.

dislike [dɪsˈlaɪk]

Andy **dislikes** vegetables.

do away [ˈduː əˈweɪ]

Jack **did away** with the giant.

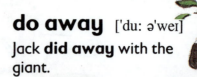

do up [ˈduː ˈʌp]

Bobby **did up** an old bike. Now it looks like new.

dress [drɛs]

Linda **dressed** as a witch for Halloween.

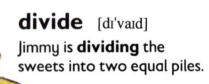

donate [dəʊˈneɪt]

Mandy **donated** her savings to the old folk's home.

divide [dɪˈvaɪd]

Jimmy is **dividing** the sweets into two equal piles.

dive [daɪv]

Bobby is **diving** into the pool.

22

drag [dræg]
The men are **dragging** the boat up onto the beach.

drift [drɪft]
There was no wind and the boat **drifted** on the sea.

drown [draʊn]
The lifeguard rescued Willy who was **drowning**.

drill [drɪl]
Uncle Roy is **drilling** a hole in the wall.

draw [drɔː]
Andy is **drawing** a rabbit.

doze [dəʊz]
Dogs love to **doze** in the sun.

drive [draɪv]
Father **drives** the car to work each morning.

drip [drɪp]
Water is **dripping** from the ceiling onto the floor.

doodle [ˈduːdl]
Helen is **doodling** on a piece of paper.

drain [dreɪn]
Kathy let the dishes **drain** after she washed them.

drink [drɪŋk]
Willy **drank** a glass of milk with breakfast.

drink up ['drɪŋk 'ʌp]
The elephant **drank up** all the water in the bucket.

dry [draɪ]
After a bath, you **dry** yourself well with a towel.

dry out ['draɪ 'aʊt]
The puddle **dried out** in the hot sun

dust [dʌst]
Mother is **dusting** the furniture.

dump [dʌmp]
The truck **dumped** the rubbish in a heap.

duck [dʌk]
The giant **ducked** his head to get through the door.

drop off ['drɒp 'ɒf]
Mother **dropped** Kathy **off** at school.

drop in ['drɒp 'ɪn]
Andy **dropped in** to see his grandmother.

drop [drɒp]
Linda **dropped** an egg on the floor.

Ee

edge [ɛdʒ]
The clown **edged** his way carefully along the narrow plank.

eat [i:t]
Elephants **eat** a lot.

eat up [ˈi:t ˈʌp]
The mouse **ate up** all the cheese.

elect [ɪˈlɛkt]
The team **elected** the captain from among themselves.

emerge [ɪˈmɜ:dʒ]
Suddenly a shark **emerged** from the water.

embrace [ɪmˈbreɪs]
Father **embraced** mother lovingly.

embarrass [ɪmˈbærəs]
Andy **embarrassed** his father by being rude in front of Aunt Molly.

earn [ɜ:n]
Bobby **earns** pocket money by washing cars.

escape [ɪˈskeɪp]
The monkey **escaped** from the cage.

engrave [ɪnˈgreɪv]
Andy is **engraving** his name in the tree trunk.

entertain [ɛntəˈteɪn]
The clown **entertained** us with his funny tricks.

enjoy [ɪnˈdʒɔɪ]
Mandy **enjoys** watching television.

enter [ˈɛntə]
The burglar is **entering** the house by the window.

employ [ɪmˈplɔɪ]
Sam is **employed** to clean windows.

empty [ˈɛmpti]
The baby **emptied** the box of blocks onto the floor.

$$1 + 1 = 2$$

equal [ˈiːkwəl]
One and one **equals** two.

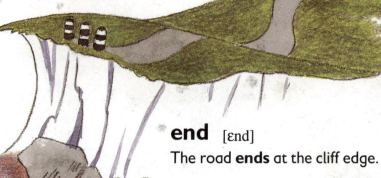

end [ɛnd]
The road **ends** at the cliff edge.

erase [ɪˈreɪz]
It is easy to **erase** mistakes with a rubber.

explain
[ɪk'spleɪn]

The teacher **explained** to the children how to jump over the hurdles.

examine [ɪg'zæmɪn]
The doctor is **examining** the sick boy.

excite
[ɪk'saɪt]

Mandy was **excited** when she saw the gold cup.

excuse [ɪk'skju:z]
Jane is **excused** from sports because she has hurt her ankle.

expand
[ɪk'spænd]

A balloon **expands** when you blow it up.

expect [ɪk'spɛkt]
I **expect** it will rain today. There are a lot of dark clouds in the sky.

exercise
['ɛksəsaɪz]

Bobby **exercises** everyday to keep fit.

explore
[ɪk'splɔ:]

Kathy is **exploring** the rock pools looking for crabs.

exchange [ɪks'tʃeɪndʒ]
Willy is **exchanging** shorts with Peter.

27

Ff

face up [ˈfeɪs ˈʌp]
It is hard to **face up** to your teacher when you have not done your homework.

face [feɪs]
Linda **faced** the clock to see what time it was.

fade [feɪd]
The curtains have **faded**.

fall [fɔːl]
Willy tripped over a stone and **fell** on his hands and knees.

fall off [ˈfɔːl ˈɒf]
Andy **fell off** his chair in fright.

faint [feɪnt]
Mandy saw a ghost and **fainted**.

fake [feɪk]
Andy **faked** a stomachache because he did not want to go to school.

fan [fæn]
Aunt Molly **fanned** herself to keep cool.

fail [feɪl]
Bobby **failed** to clear the high jump.

fast [fɑ:st]
The holy man is **fasting**.
He is not eating any food.

farm [fɑ:m]
Uncle Roy **farms** a small piece of land behind the house.

feed [fi:d]
Simon **feeds** his pet rabbit carrots and lettuce.

feel [fi:l]
Rabbits **feel** soft and cuddly.

fear [fɪə]
Kathy **fears** snakes.

fetch [fɛtʃ]
The dog **fetches** the stick for Jimmy.

feel like ['fi:l laɪk]
On a hot day we **feel like** a cold drink.

fasten ['fɑ:sn]
Willy is **fastening** his seat belt.

find [faɪnd]
Mandy **found** a coin on the footpath.

find out ['faɪnd 'aʊt]
Jimmy looked in the phone book to **find out** Peter's phone number.

fit [fɪt]
Cinderella's foot **fitted** the shoe perfectly.

fit in ['fɪt ɪn]
Only five people could **fit in** the car.

finish ['fɪnɪʃ]
The rabbit **finished** first in the race.

finish with ['fɪnɪʃ wɪð]
Helen had **finished with** the book, so she returned it to the library.

fill [fɪl]
Andy is **filling** the pool with water.

fill up ['fɪl 'ʌp]
Jane **filled up** the bucket with sand.

fence [fɛns]
Uncle Roy is **fencing** the tree with wire.

fight [faɪt]
Bobby and Jimmy are **fighting**.

film [fɪlm]
They are **filming** a fight.

flap [flæp]

The washing is **flapping** in the wind.

flag [flæg]

The people **flag** the buildings to celebrate the king's birthday.

flag down ['flæg 'daʊn]

We **flag down** a taxi.

flash [flæʃ]

The light from the lighthouse **flashed** across the sea.

flow [fləʊ]

The river **flows** down to the sea.

float [fləʊt]

Kathy can **float** on her back.

flood [flʌd]

Andy left the tap on and **flooded** the floor.

flush [flʌʃ]

Jane is **flushing** the toilet.

fizz [fɪz]
This drink **fizzes** for a while when I pour it out.

flatten [ˈflætn]
Willy **flattened** the plasticine.

fold [fəʊld]
Andy **folded** a piece of paper to make a dart.

flip [flɪp]
I can **flip** a coin in the air.

fix [fɪks]
Helen is **fixing** lunch.

freeze [fri:z]
When water **freezes** it becomes ice.

fling [flɪŋ]
The lazy boy **flung** his clothes on the floor.

foam [fəʊm]
The beer **foams** over the glass.

form [fɔ:m]
Jimmy **forms** a K with his body.

forget [fəˈgɛt]
Poor Willy cannot write. He has **forgotten** to bring his pencil.

frown [fraʊn]
Bobby **frowns** when he is worried.

fire ['faɪə]

The hunter is **firing** at the birds.

fly [flaɪ]

Birds **fly** in the sky.

fish [fɪʃ]

Jimmy likes to **fish** with his father.

flick [flɪk]

The cow is **flicking** the flies with its tail.

fluff [flʌf]

The hen is **fluffing** out its feathers.

flit [flɪt]

The butterfly **flits** from flower to flower.

flee [fli:]

The animals are **fleeing** from the burning forest.

free [fri:]

Linda is **freeing** the bird from its cage.

follow ['fɒləu]

The dog **followed** Jimmy home from school.

Gg

frighten ['fraɪtn]
Little Miss Muffet was **frightened** by the spider.

gallop ['gæləp]
Jimmy was afraid when his horse **galloped** down the hill.

gamble ['gæmbl]
These men are **gambling**.

fry [fraɪ]
Mother is **frying** an egg for Andy.

garden ['gɑːdn]
Father is **gardening**. He is planting roses.

gather ['gæðə]
Grandfather **gathered** fruit from the trees.

furnish ['fɜːnɪʃ]
Aunt Molly **furnished** her room with a bed, dressing table and chair.

gasp [gɑːsp]
The water was so cold, Bobby **gasped** with shock.

gaze [geɪz]
Kathy is **gazing** at the stars.

give [gɪv]
Mother **gave** Andy a bag.

give away [ˈgɪv əˈweɪ]
Jimmy didn't want his pencils so he **gave** them **away**.

give up [ˈgɪv ˈʌp]
The robber **gave** himself **up** to the police.

give back [ˈgɪv ˈbæk]
The teacher is **giving back** the exercise books.

give out [ˈgɪv ˈaʊt]
The headmaster is **giving out** prizes to the best pupils.

give off [ˈgɪv ˈɒf]
A fire **gives off** smoke.

glue [gluː]
Kathy **glued** a picture in the book.

glare [glɛə]
The two boys have stopped fighting, but they are still **glaring**.

glow [gləʊ]
The cat's eyes **glow** in the dark.

get off ['gɛt 'ɒf]
Bobby **got off** the bus at the swimming pool.

get around ['gɛt ə'raʊnd]
Pilots **get around** a lot.
They visit many countries.

get up ['gɛt 'ʌp]
Andy **gets up** at 7 o'clock.

get in ['gɛt 'ɪn]
Ali Baba **got in** a jar to hide from the thieves.

get dressed ['gɛt 'drɛst]
It is late.
You must **get dressed** at once.

giggle ['gɪgl]
The playful puppy made Kathy **giggle**.

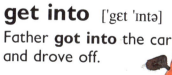

get into ['gɛt 'ɪntə]
Father **got into** the car and drove off.

get along ['gɛt ə'lɒŋ]
Helen is a sweet girl who **gets along** with all her classmates.

go [gəʊ]
Andy **goes** for a drive in his toy car.

glide [glaɪd]
A paper aeroplane **glides** through the air.

go back [ˈgəʊ ˈbæk]
Linda forgot her umbrella. She **went back** home for it.

go out [ˈgəʊ ˈaʊt]
Mr and Mrs Brown are **going out** to a party.

go away [ˈgəʊ əˈweɪ]
"**Go away!**" said Jane. "I want to be alone."

go on [ˈgəʊ ɒn]
Mandy **went on** the roller coaster.

go without [ˈgəʊ wɪðˈaʊt]
Andy was naughty and had to **go without** dinner.

grill [grɪl]
Father is **grilling** some sausages.

grip [grɪp]
Kathy **gripped** her mother's arm when they were on the ferris wheel.

grin [grɪn]
Willy is **grinning** because his mother has given him a toy.

grind [graɪnd]
The cook is **grinding** nuts.

grab [græb]
The thief **grabbed** Aunt Molly's handbag.

growl [graʊl]
The guard dog **growled** at the stranger.

grow [grəʊ]
Potatoes **grow** under the ground.

grunt [grʌnt]
When pigs are hungry they **grunt**.

group [gruːp]
Simon **grouped** the toy animals into pets and wild animals.

greet [griːt]
We **greeted** Grandmother with a bunch of flowers.

guard [gɑːd]
The soldiers **guard** the jewels from thieves.

guide [gaɪd]
The boy scout **guided** the blind man across the street.

gush [gʌʃ]
Look! The water is **gushing** out of the broken pipe.

guess [gɛs]
Close your eyes and **guess** what your present is.

gum [gʌm]
Linda **gummed** the two cards together to make a thicker card.

Hh

hack [hæk]
The fireman **hacked** the door with an axe.

halt [hɔ:lt]
"**Halt!**" said the fireman. "You cannot enter."

halve [ha:v]
Mandy **halved** the orange before squeezing out the juice.

handle ['hændl]
Linda **handled** the glasses with great care.

handcuff ['hændkʌf]
The policeman **handcuffed** the thief.

hail [heɪl]
Aunt Molly **hailed** a taxi to take her home.

hammer ['hæmə]
Jimmy **hammered** a nail into the wood.

hand [hænd]
The postman **handed** the letter to Kathy.

hand out ['hænd 'aʊt]
Mother is **handing out** sweets to the children.

hang [hæŋ]
Andy **hung** his shirt up in the cupboard.

has ['hæz] or [həz]
Jimmy **has** a blue cap.

has got [həz 'gɒt]
Willy **has got** chicken pox.

has to ['hæz tə]
We **have to** drink water everyday.

harvest ['hɑːvɪst]
The farmer is **harvesting** the crop.

hatch [hætʃ]
The chicks **hatched** out of the eggs.

hate [heɪt]
Willy **hates** to wake up early on cold mornings.

heal [hiːl]
The cut on my arm has **healed**. I can take off the plaster.

harm [hɑːm]
Is the big bad wolf going to **harm** Red Riding Hood?

haul [hɔːl]
The fishermen **hauled** their net onto the boat.

hoot [hu:t]
Owls **hoot** at night.

hook [hʊk]
Jimmy has **hooked** a big fish.

honk [hɒŋk]
Geese **honk** at strangers.

hum [hʌm]
Willy is **humming** as he walks to the park.

hop [hɒp]
The children are **hopping** around the playground.

hurl [hɜ:l]
Jimmy **hurled** the ball as far as he could.

hurt [hɜ:t]
Simon **hurt** his toe on a rock.

huff [hʌf]
The children **huffed** and puffed after the run.

huddle ['hʌdl]
The chicks are **huddling** together to keep warm.

hose [həʊz]

Father is **hosing** the car down.

howl [haʊl]

The baby **howled** when it fell out of its cot.

hurry [ˈhʌri]

Jimmy got up late and **hurried** to get dressed.

hurry up [ˈhʌri ˈʌp]

Hurry up if you want to get to school on time!

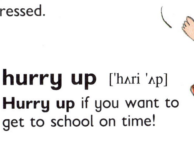

hunt [hʌnt]

Grandmother is **hunting** for her glasses.

hug [hʌg]

Mother **hugs** me when I come home from school.

hush [hʌʃ]

Hush! Don't wake the baby.

Ii

imitate ['ɪmɪteɪt]
Willy can **imitate** Superman very well.

inspect [ɪn'spɛkt]
Bobby dropped his kite. He **inspected** it to make sure that it was all right.

injure ['ɪndʒə]
Simon fell down and **injured** his arm.

inform [ɪn'fɔːm]
The teacher **informed** the children where to go to fly their kites.

itch [ɪtʃ]
Peter's arm **itches** because a mosquito bit him there.

invent [ɪn'vɛnt]
The scientist **invented** a machine to walk a dog.

imagine [ɪ'mædʒɪn]
Kathy **imagined** she was a movie star.

Jj

judge [dʒʌdʒ]
Kathy's dog was **judged** the best dog in the show.

join [dʒɔɪn]
Willy can **join** two pieces of string with a knot.

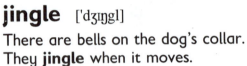

jingle ['dʒɪŋgl]
There are bells on the dog's collar. They **jingle** when it moves.

jump to ['dʒʌmp tə]
The dogs **jumped to** attention when the judge arrived.

jump [dʒʌmp]
The cat **jumped** over the sleeping dog and ran off as quickly as it could.

jump at ['dʒʌmp ət]
The dog **jumped at** the man passing by.

jump up ['dʒʌmp ˌʌp]
Puss **jumped up** on to Andy's lap.

jack up ['dʒæk 'ʌp]
Father **jacked up** the car to change the tyre.

jerk [dʒɜ:k]
The car **jerked** a few times and then stopped suddenly.

joke [dʒəuk]
The children are **joking** with one another.
They are telling funny stories.

jumble ['dʒʌmbl]
The naughty girl **jumbled** her clothes up.

juggle ['dʒʌgl]
The clown is **juggling** six balls.

jam [dʒæm]
Andy **jammed** the clothes in the suitcase.

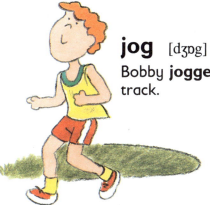

jog [dʒɒg]
Bobby **jogged** around the track.

jot [dʒɒt]
Peter **jotted** down my phone number on a piece of paper.

Kk

kick [kɪk]
Terry **kicked** the ball over the fence.

keep [ki:p]
Helen **keeps** her pet snake in a basket.

keep up [ˈki:p ˈʌp]
Bobby can run faster than Willy. Willy can't **keep up** with him.

keep away [ˈki:p əˈweɪ]
Keep away from the dog. It bites!

keep off [ˈki:p ˈɒf]
Keep off the grass. There are prickles.

knock [nɒk]
The postman is **knocking** on the door. He has a parcel to deliver.

kill [kɪl]
The prince became a hero when he **killed** a dragon.

kneel [ni:l]
Jimmy **kneels** down to pray.

kiss [kɪs]
Mother **kissed** Kathy on her cheek.

knit [nɪt]
Grandmother is **knitting** a jumper.

knot [nɒt]
Mandy is **knotting** a scarf round her neck.

know [nəʊ]
Peter **knows** the answer to the sum.

Ll

ladle [ˈleɪdl]
The old woman is **ladling** out soup to the children.

leap [li:p]
Helen opened the box and a frog **leapt** out.

laugh [lɑ:f]
Andy is **laughing** because Jane is tickling him.

laugh at [ˈlɑ:f ət]
The children are **laughing at** the clown's tricks.

learn [lɜːn]

Jane is **learning** how to play the piano.

let [lɛt]

The teacher **let** Andy play the guitar.

lend [lɛnd]

Mandy **lent** Linda her music book.

let down ['lɛt 'daʊn]

Rapunzel **let down** her long hair.

like [laɪk]

Jimmy **likes** the trumpet. Kathy **likes** the flute.

let go ['lɛt 'gəʊ]

Bobby **let go** of the balloon and it floated away.

listen ['lɪsn]

Andy is **listening** to the radio.

let in ['lɛt 'ɪn]

Open the door and **let** Simon **in**.

let out ['lɛt 'aʊt]

Willy **let out** a cry of pain when he hit his finger.

53

lie [laɪ]
Andy is **lying**.

The cat is **lying** in the washing basket.

lie down ['laɪ 'daʊn]
Grandmother is tired.
She is **lying down** on the sofa.

light [laɪt]
Grandfather is very careful when he **lights** the candle.

link [lɪŋk]
The new road **links** the two towns.

lose [luːz]
Jimmy dropped $10 and **lost** it.

list [lɪst]
Aunt Molly is **listing** the things she needs to buy.

limp [lɪmp]
The dog has a sore paw and is **limping**.

lift [lɪft]
Willy **lifted** Jimmy up.

lick [lɪk]
Andy is **licking** a lollipop.

litter [ˈlɪtə]
Andy has **littered** the floor with sweet wrappers.

long [lɒŋ]
Andy is **longing** for chocolate. It's his favourite food.

line [laɪn]
Kathy is **lining** the shelf with paper.

line up [ˈlaɪn ˈʌp]
Mandy **lined up** the chairs for the concert.

loll [lɒl]
Willy is **lolling** on the sofa, doing nothing.

live [lɪv]
There was an old woman who **lived** in a shoe.

live on [ˈlɪv ɒn]
Monkeys **live on** fruit and nuts.

55

look [lʊk]
Look at the aeroplane flying upside down.

look out ['lʊk 'aʊt]
Look out! A branch is falling down.

look after ['lʊk 'ɑːftə]
Mother **looks after** the baby all day.

look for ['lʊk fə]
The children are **looking for** the lost ball.

look up ['lʊk 'ʌp]
Helen doesn't know how to spell a word.
She is **looking** it **up** in the dictionary.

lock up ['lɒk 'ʌp]
Aunt Molly **locks up** her jewels in a safe.

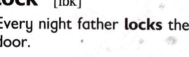

lock [lɒk]
Every night father **locks** the door.

load [ləʊd]
The men are **loading** the van with sacks of flour.

56

loop [lu:p]
The cowboy **loops** the rope round the bull.

Mm

mail [meɪl]
Kathy has written a letter to her friend. She is **mailing** it.

mount [maʊnt]
Bobby is **mounting** his bicycle.

love [lʌv]
I **love** my grandmother.

mark [mɑ:k]
The teacher is **marking** the exercise books.

mow [məʊ]
Father is **mowing** the lawn.

lunch [lʌntʃ]
Andy is **lunching** with his aunt.

mash [mæʃ]
Jimmy is **mashing** the potatoes.

measure ['mɛʒə]
Andy is **measuring** the flour with a cup.

melt [mɛlt]
Ice **melts** when you take it out of the freezer.

make of ['meɪk əv]
This jar is **made of** glass.

make [meɪk]
Willy is **making** a sandwich for himself.

make off ['meɪk 'ɒf]
The thief **made off** with a big cake.

make from ['meɪk frəm]
This jam is **made from** strawberries.

make out ['meɪk 'aʊt]
The stranger wore a mask and Helen couldn't **make out** who he was.

make for ['meɪk fə]
Jimmy **made for** the door when Linda ran after him with a rolling pin.

mince [mɪns]

Simon is **mincing** the meat to make pies.

mix [mɪks]

Willy **mixed** flour and water to make a dough.

mend [mɛnd]

Bobby is **mending** the broken toaster.

mistake [mɪˈsteɪk]

Andy **mistook** pepper for salt.

mess up [ˈmɛs ˌʌp]

The wind **messed up** Kathy's hair.

mew [mju:]

The cat is **mewing**. It wants food.

mop [mɒp]

Peter is **mopping** the floor to clean off his dirty footprints.

mime [maɪm]

Andy is **miming** that he wants a drink.

match [mætʃ]
Jimmy's socks do not **match**.

model ['mɒdl]
Kathy is **modelling** a party dress.

marry ['mæri]
Aunt Jane **married** a soldier.

miss [mɪs]
The paper aeroplane just **missed** Linda's head.

miss out ['mɪs 'aʊt]
When the teacher was giving the children crayons, he **missed out** Willy.

mask [mɑːsk]
The children **mask** their faces for the party.

meet [miːt]
Bobby **met** Mandy outside the post office.

march [mɑːtʃ]
The band **marched** down the street playing music.

moo [muː]
Cows **moo**.

milk [mɪlk]
The farmer is **milking** the cow.

mine [maɪn]
The miners are **mining** coal from under the ground.

move [muːv]
Jimmy picked up his books and **moved** them to another desk.

move in [ˈmuːv ˈɪn]
Mr and Mrs Sharp are **moving in** next door.

move out [ˈmuːv ˈaʊt]
Bobby is **moving out** of the haunted house.

nibble ['nɪbl]

The mouse is **nibbling** at the bread.

name [neɪm]

The baby was **named** Melissa Anne.

net [nɛt]

Jimmy has **netted** a big fish.

nurse [nɜːs]

Mother **nursed** Andy when he had measles.

Oo

overturn [ˌəʊvəˈtɜːn]

The boat **overturned** in the storm.

owe [əʊ]

Peter borrows $1 from Jimmy.
He **owes** Jimmy $1.

open [ˈəʊpən]

Linda is **opening** her birthday presents.

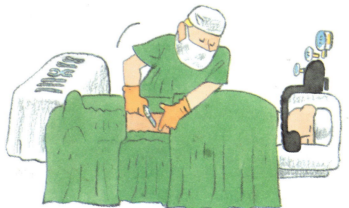

operate [ˈɒpəreɪt]

The surgeon is **operating** on a man who has broken his leg.

overtake [ˌəʊvəˈteɪk]
Our car is **overtaking** the truck.

order [ˈɔːdə]
Kathy **ordered** a hamburger and french fries for lunch.

oil [ɔɪl]
Andy **oiled** the wheels of his toy car.

offer [ˈɒfə]
Bobby **offered** to help Helen repair her bicycle.

own [əʊn]
Mandy saved up her money and now **owns** a new bicycle.

obey [əˈbeɪ]
Mother said, 'Go to bed' and I had to **obey**.

occupy [ˈɒkjupaɪ]
Peter wanted to use the bathroom but it was **occupied**.

Pp

pierce [pɪəs]
The arrow **pierced** the apple.

paddle ['pædl]
Bobby is **paddling** the canoe down the river.

pack [pæk]
Kathy is **packing** food for a picnic.

picnic ['pɪknɪk]
The children are **picnicking** by the river.

pack up ['pæk 'ʌp]
The picnic is over.
The children are **packing up** the things.

peel [pi:l]
Linda is **peeling** the orange.

peck [pɛk]
The little bird is **pecking** at the apple.

poke [pəuk]
Andy is **poking** a stick into the sand.

pluck [plʌk]
Jimmy is busy **plucking** apples.

parachute [ˈpærəʃuːt]
Linda is **parachuting** into the forest.

pedal [ˈpɛdl]
Bobby is **pedalling** his new bicycle up the hill.

peep [piːp]
Mandy is **peeping** through the window.

photograph [ˈfəʊtəgrɑːf]
Jimmy is **photographing** the playful kitten.

pose [pəʊz]
Andy is **posing** for a photograph.

perch [pɜːtʃ]
The bird has **perched** on a branch.

pant [pænt]
The dog is **panting** after running up the steep slope.

pat [pæt]
Linda is **patting** the dog on the head.

paw [pɔː]
The dog is **pawing** the rubber bone.

perform [pəˈfɔːm]
The magician is **performing** a trick.

park [pɑːk]

Mother **parked** the car next to a van.

patch [pætʃ]

Mother is **patching** a hole in the knee of Andy's jeans.

plant [plɑːnt]

Mother is **planting** some daisy seeds in the garden.

pay [peɪ]

Father is **paying** for the groceries at the check-out counter.

pay back ['peɪ 'bæk]

Jimmy is **paying back** the ten dollars Peter lent him.

prepare [prɪ'pɛə]

Father is **preparing** the fruit for dinner He is cutting it.

peg [pɛg]

Mother is **pegging** her washing.

present [prɪ'zɛnt]

Andy is **presenting** his mother with a bunch of roses.

place [pleɪs]

Mother **placed** the antique vase on the mantlepiece.

paint [peɪnt]
Andy is **painting** a picture of his family.

paste [peɪst]
Bobby is **pasting** a poster on the wall.

pin [pɪn]
Our teacher **pinned** a notice on the noticeboard.

pair [pɛə]
The socks are all mixed up. Can you **pair** them again?

part [pɑːt]
Terry always **parts** his hair on the left.

praise [preɪz]
The teacher is **praising** Peter for the improvement in his school work.

punish [ˈpʌnɪʃ]
Andy was **punished** for being naughty.

play [pleɪ]
Mandy and Kathy are **playing** hopscotch in the playground.

pretend [prɪˈtɛnd]
Willy is **pretending** to be a ghost.

pound [paʊnd]
Mother is **pounding** the meat to make it tender.

pass [pɑːs]
Jimmy is **passing** the salt to Linda.

powder [ˈpaʊdə]
Aunt Molly is **powdering** her face.

pinch [pɪntʃ]
A monster sneaked up and **pinched** my arm.

pile [paɪl]
Jane is **piling** up the sand to make a sandcastle.

pick [pɪk]
Jimmy is **picking** mangoes from a tree in his garden.

pick out [ˈpɪk ˈaʊt]
Mandy has **picked out** all the black jelly beans.

patrol [pəˈtrəʊl]
Two policemen are **patrolling** our street.

pick up [ˈpɪk ˈʌp]
Willy is **picking up** the pieces of broken glass.

polish [ˈpɒlɪʃ]

Father has washed the car. He is now **polishing** it.

plough [plaʊ]

The farmer **ploughs** his field before planting corn.

protect [prəˈtɛkt]

The shell of the snail **protects** it from harm.

pave [peɪv]

The workmen are **paving** the road.

press [prɛs]

Press this button to start the machine.

prick [prɪk]

A thorn **pricked** her finger when Helen was cutting the roses.

pull [pʊl]

The elephant is **pulling** the log out of the forest.

pull down [ˈpʊl ˈdaʊn]

The workman is **pulling down** the house.

pull out [ˈpʊl ˈaʊt]

Andy's tooth was loose, so the dentist **pulled** it **out**.

pour [pɔː]
Aunt Molly is **pouring** the tea into the cups.

pour on [ˈpɔːr ɒn]
Jimmy **poured** water **on** the fire to put it out.

purr [pɜː]
Our cat **purrs** when you pat her.

pounce [paʊns]
The cat **pounced** on the mouse.

promise [ˈprɒmɪs]
'I **promise** to look after it well,' said Simon.
'I will feed it and clean it.'

point [pɔɪnt]
Andy is **pointing** a finger at the puppies that chewed his father's slippers.

point out [ˈpɔɪnt ˈaʊt]
The guide **pointed out** the old tower to the tourists.

post [pəʊst]
Kathy **posted** a letter to her French penpal.

pump [pʌmp]
Bobby **pumps** up his bicycle tyre.

71

practise ['præktɪs]
Kathy **practises** hard for a ballet performance.

push [pʊʃ]
Jimmy is **pushing** the box up the hill.

put [pʊt]
Peter is **putting** his coins into his money box.

put away ['pʊt ə'weɪ]
Helen **puts away** her toys after playing with them.

Qq

quack [kwæk]
The ducks **quack** when the farmer comes to feed them.

print [prɪnt]
The machine **prints** posters.

puzzle ['pʌzl]
The men **puzzled** over the huge footprint in the snow.

question ['kwɛstʃən]
The policeman **questioned** Jimmy to find out how the accident happened.

Rr

quarter [ˈkwɔːtə]
Aunt Molly **quartered** the cake.

quarrel [ˈkwɒrəl]
Mandy and Helen are **quarrelling** over the torn storybook.

reach [riːtʃ]
Linda can't **reach** the book on top of the bookcase.

queue up [ˈkjuː ˈʌp]
The children are **queuing up** to return their library books.

renew [rɪˈnjuː]
Willy had not finished his book, so he took it to the library and **renewed** it.

read [riːd]
Andy is **reading** Treasure Island.

raise [reɪz]
Peter has **raised** his hand. He knows the answer to the question.

relate [rɪˈleɪt]
Grandfather **related** the story of his childhood.

record [rɪˈkɔːd]
Kathy **recorded** the day's events in her diary.

rush [rʌʃ]
The ambulance is **rushing** a very sick man to hospital.

rain [reɪn]
It is **raining** very heavily so we cannot go outside.

report [rɪ'pɔːt]
Uncle Roy **reported** to the police that his truck was stolen.

reverse [rɪ'vɜːs]
Mother is **reversing** the car. Get out of the way!

ram [ræm]
Uncle Roy's truck **rammed** a bus.

repair [rɪ'pɛə]
Our car would not start. The mechanic is **repairing** it.

replace [rɪ'pleɪs]
The mechanic **replaced** the spanner after he had used it. He put it back into the tool box.

run [rʌn]
Rusty can **run** very fast.

run out of ['rʌn 'aʊt əv]
The car **ran out of** petrol in the middle of the road.

run into ['rʌn 'ɪntə]
The car **ran into** a lamp-post.

run over ['rʌn 'əʊvə]
The car **ran over** a watermelon and squashed it.

run away ['rʌn ə'weɪ]
The thief is **running away** with the jewels.

run after ['rʌn 'ɑːftə]
Bobby **ran after** the thief, trying to catch him.

run in ['rʌn 'ɪn]
The thief was **run in** for stealing the jewels.

request [rɪ'kwɛst]
Hospital visitors are **requested** to leave by nine o'clock in the evening.

refuse [rɪˈfjuːz]
The camel **refuses** to stand up.

remind [rɪˈmaɪnd]
The tall, thin man **reminds** Mandy of a giraffe.

race [reɪs]
The hare and the tortoise are **racing** against each other.

ride [raɪd]
Jimmy **rides** a horse very well.

release [rɪˈliːs]
Linda is **releasing** the rabbit from the cage.

roar [rɔː]
The lion is **roaring** because he is angry.

repeat [rɪˈpiːt]
The parrot is **repeating** the same word over and over again.

receive [rɪˈsiːv]
Andy **received** many presents on his birthday.

remove [rɪˈmuːv]
Peter is **removing** his dirty boots.

rake [reɪk]
Grandfather is **raking** the leaves into a pile.

reflect [rɪˈflɛkt]
The moon is **reflected** in the lake.

regret [rɪˈgrɛt]
Andy **regrets** that he can't go on the picnic. He is sick.

reserve [rɪˈzɜːv]
This table is **reserved** for the Brown family.

rescue [ˈrɛskjuː]
The fireman **rescued** Jane from the fire.

ruffle [ˈrʌfl]
Uncle Roy is **ruffling** Jimmy's hair.

reveal [rɪˈviːl]
The artist removed the sheet and **revealed** the statue.

respect [rɪˈspɛkt]
Jimmy **respects** old people and gives them his seat on the bus.

ruin [ˈruːɪn]
The painting was left out in the rain and was **ruined**.

reply [rɪ'plaɪ]
'What's your name?' asked the robot.
'Andy,' I **replied**.

remain [rɪ'meɪn]
Willy had four sweets. He had eaten three. One **remains**.

remember [rɪ'membə]
Father **remembered** it was mother's birthday.

row [rəʊ]
Jimmy is **rowing** the boat across the lake.

roller-skate ['rəʊləskeɪt]
Bobby is **roller-skating** down the path.

rest [rɛst]
After hiking all day, Linda is **resting** her feet.

rub [rʌb]
Willy **rubs** himself dry after his shower.

result [rɪ'zʌlt]
The race **resulted** in a tie. Bobby and Terry shared the first prize.

rip [rɪp]
The naughty dog is **ripping** the curtain to pieces.

rub out ['rʌb 'aʊt]
Mandy made a mistake but she **rubbed** it **out**.

rule [ru:l]
The king **rules** his country wisely.

roam [rəʊm]
The girls are **roaming** around the park, looking at the flowers here and there.

Ss

sag [sæg]
The top shelf **sags** because the books are too heavy.

rob [rɒb]
The thieves are **robbing** the man of his money.

scold [skəʊld]
The teacher is **scolding** Jimmy because he has not done his homework.

scream [skri:m]
Mandy **screamed** when a bee landed on her arm.

scrub [skrʌb]
We **scrub** the floors to get them clean.

shape [ʃeɪp]
The potter is **shaping** the clay to make a pot.

screw [skru:]
Uncle Roy is **screwing** the shelf to the wall.

80

save [seɪv]
Terry **saves** ten cents from his pocket money every day.

save up [ˈseɪv ˈʌp]
He wants to **save up** enough money to buy a pair of roller skates.

salute [səˈluːt]
The children are **saluting** the flag.

score [skɔː]
Bobby **scored** a goal for his team.

scrape [skreɪp]
Jimmy fell down and **scraped** his knee.

scratch [skrætʃ]
The cat is **scratching** the flag pole to sharpen her claws.

scratch out [ˈskrætʃ ˈaʊt]
Kathy is **scratching out** the words so that no one can read them.

search [sɜːtʃ]
Linda is **searching** everywhere to find the lost crayon.

select [səˈlɛkt]
The judge **selected** the best painting in the show.

send [sɛnd]
Mother **sent** Andy to buy some sugar.

send back ['sɛnd 'bæk]
Rusty followed Kathy to school so she **sent** him **back** home.

send off ['sɛnd 'ɒf]
The soccer player was **sent off** the field for kicking another player.

sell [sɛl]
Simon helped his father **sell** oranges.

sell out ['sɛl 'aʊt]
The oranges **sold out** in an hour.
There were none left.

set [sɛt]
Andy is **setting** the table for dinner.

set about ['sɛt ə'baʊt]
Andy **set about** his homework right after dinner.

set down ['sɛt 'daʊn]
Willy **set down** his books on the desk.

set off ['sɛt 'ɒf]
The boys **set off** on their hike at daybreak.

84

shear [ʃɪə]
The farmer is **shearing** a sheep.

shine [ʃaɪn]
Jimmy **shines** his shoes every morning before school.

seal [siːl]
Peter put the letter in the envelope and **sealed** it.

sign [saɪn]
Peter **signed** his name at the bottom of the letter.

shock [ʃɒk]
The news **shocked** Mandy. She didn't expect such a terrible thing to happen.

show [ʃəʊ]
The salesman is **showing** Kathy some shoes.

shop [ʃɒp]
Linda is **shopping** for a pair of sunglasses.

show off [ˌʃəʊ ˈɒf]
Kathy is **showing off** her new shoes.

show up [ˌʃəʊ ˈʌp]
Jimmy **showed up** only after Helen had waited for him for an hour.

shake [ʃeɪk]
Andy is **shaking** the medicine bottle to mix the medicine.

shake off [ˈʃeɪk ˈɒf]
A spider landed on Mandy's hand but she **shook** it **off**.

separate [ˈsɛpəreɪt]
Mother is **separating** the egg yolk from the egg white.

serve [sɜːv]
Kathy is **serving** drinks to her guests.

sharpen [ˈʃɑːpən]
Father is **sharpening** the carving knife carefully.

sit [sɪt]
Andy is **sitting** on the bean bag.

sit down [ˈsɪt ˈdaʊn]
Jimmy **sat down** and watched television.

sew [səʊ]
Grandmother **sewed** the button on my jacket.

sit up [ˈsɪt ˈʌp]
The teacher told Andy to **sit up** and pay attention.

sit back [ˈsɪt ˈbæk]
Grandfather **sits back** while Kathy does the work.

shift [ʃɪft]

Willy is **shifting** the armchair closer to the fireplace.

soak [səʊk]

Bobby is **soaking** his sore feet in a bucket of hot water.

smooth [smuːð]

Kathy is **smoothing** out the wrinkles on the bed.

shower [ˈʃaʊə]

You are dirty! Go and **shower**.

sing [sɪŋ]

Andy likes to **sing** in the shower.

shell [ʃɛl]

Linda is **shelling** the nuts for the fruit cake.

shut [ʃʌt]

Kathy is **shutting** the window because the rain is coming in.

shut up [ˈʃʌt ˈʌp]

Andy has been talking for an hour.
His brother is getting tired and says, 'Please **shut up**!'

snore [snɔː]

Grandfather **snores** when he sleeps.

slope [sləup]
The path is **sloping** up the hill.

slide [slaɪd]
Bobby is **sliding** down the hill on a tyre.

spin [spɪn]
Can you **spin** on a frozen pond?

sniff [snɪf]
The dog **sniffed** out the rabbit.

surpise [sə'praɪz]
Andy **surprised** Mandy when he jumped out from behind the snowman.

snow [snəu]
It **snows** in winter and you can make a snowman.

sneeze [sni:z]
Willy **sneezes** all the time because he has a cold.

support [sə'pɔ:t]
We **supported** Willy on each side and helped him off the snow.

stare [stɛə]
Linda is **staring** at the chick in amazement.

shoot [ʃuːt]
Bobby **shoots** at the target twice.

shelter [ˈʃɛltə]
The sheep **sheltered** from the rain under the tree.

slip [slɪp]
The clown **slipped** on the banana skin.

stink [stɪŋk]
The rotting fish **stinks**.

spell [spɛl]
Linda can **spell** her name.

slip off [ˈslɪp ˈɒf]
Jimmy **slipped off** his shoes before entering the house.

slip under [ˈslɪp ˈʌndə]
Mandy is **slipping** a letter **under** the door.

snatch [snætʃ]
Andy **snatched** the toy from his sister.

slice [slaɪs]
Aunt Molly is **slicing** some bread for lunch.

smash [smæʃ]
Willy dropped a glass and it **smashed** onto the floor.

spray [spreɪ]
Grandfather is **spraying** water on the plants.

sow [səʊ]
Andy **sows** the seeds in the garden.

sweep [swi:p]
Jimmy is **sweeping** the leaves from the path.

sprinkle ['sprɪŋkl]
Kathy is **sprinkling** water on the flowers.

see [si:]
Willy **sees** a caterpillar on the leaf.

spot [spɒt]
Simon **spotted** a bug on another leaf.

swallow ['swɒləʊ]
The snake **swallowed** a whole chicken.

sting [stɪŋ]
A bee **stung** Mandy on the finger.

smell [smɛl]
Smell this and tell me what it is.

swell [swɛl]
Mandy's finger **swelled** up after a bee stung her there.

spill [spɪl]
The baby knocked its plate over and the food **spilt** onto the floor.

spring [sprɪŋ]
The jack-in-the-box lid **sprang** open, making the baby laugh.

spoon [spu:n]
Mother is **spooning** food into the baby's mouth.

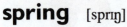

sleep [sli:p]
Babies look sweet when they are **sleeping**.

speak [spi:k]
Speak softly! Baby is sleeping.

stuff [stʌf]
Mother is **stuffing** the pillow with feathers.

smile [smaɪl]
The baby **smiled** when it saw its father.

spit [spɪt]
The food tasted awful so Andy **spat** it out.

spank [spæŋk]
Father **spanked** Andy for tearing the book.

speed [spi:d]

Uncle Roy is **speeding** around the race track on his motorbike. See how fast he goes.

spend [spɛnd]

Jimmy has **spent** all his money. He has no money left.

split [splɪt]

Father **split** the wood with an axe

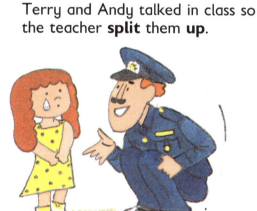

split up [ˈsplɪt ˈʌp]

Terry and Andy talked in class so the teacher **split** them **up**.

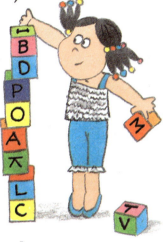

stack [stæk]

Mandy is **stacking** her building blocks.

steer [stɪə]

You **steer** a horse with the reins.

squat [skwɒt]

The policeman **squats** down to talk to the little lost girl.

squash [skwɒʃ]

Andy's car ran over a ball and **squashed** it.

spoil [spɔɪl]

Willy's parents **spoil** him. They put the television and video recorder in his room.

store [stɔː]
The boxes are **stored** in the attic.

shave [ʃeɪv]
Father **shaves** every morning.

squeeze [skwiːz]
Willy is **squeezing** out some toothpaste.

shampoo [ʃæmˈpuː]
Kathy is **shampooing** her hair.

stay [steɪ]
Grandfather has come to **stay** with us for the weekend.

stay up [ˈsteɪ ˈʌp]
Andy **stayed up** till midnight to finish reading the ghost story.

stay in [ˈsteɪ ˈɪn]
Helen had to **stay in** after school to do her homework.

stay out [ˈsteɪ ˈaʊt]
The boys **stayed out** in the garden all night.

stay away [ˈsteɪ əˈweɪ]
'**Stay away** from the fire,' said Aunt Molly. 'You might get burnt.'

steal [sti:l]

The burglar is **stealing** the silver.

sound [saʊnd]

The alarm clock **sounded** at six o'clock.

start [stɑ:t]

Grandmother **started** knitting a jumper but she hasn't finished it yet.

stretch [strɛtʃ]

Willy gets out of bed and **stretches** himself.

stick [stɪk]

Kathy is **sticking** a stamp on the envelope.

stoop [stu:p]

Andy **stoops** down to pick up the pencil.

stir [stɜ:]

Kathy is **stirring** the soup on the stove.

stick up [ˈstɪk ˈʌp]

'**Stick up** your hands!' said the robber.

stick out [ˈstɪk ˈaʊt]

Andy is **sticking out** his tongue at his friend.

stick together [ˈstɪk təˈgɛðə]

The pieces of the broken vase have been **stuck together** with glue.

stand for ['stænd fə]
What colour **stands for** danger?

stand [stænd]
Andy **stands** on the stool to reach the cookie jar.

stand back ['stænd 'bæk]
The policeman told everyone to **stand back** from the monster.

stitch [stɪtʃ]
Grandmother **stitched** a pretty bow on the collar of the dress.

stand up ['stænd 'ʌp]
Stand up and give your seat to the old gentleman.

stitch up ['stɪtʃ 'ʌp]
My hem came undone, so I **stitched** it **up**.

stop [stɒp]
Our car **stopped** at the red light.

stop up ['stɒp 'ʌp]
Bobby **stopped up** the hole in the wall with cardboard.

string [strɪŋ]
Linda is **stringing** the beads to make a necklace.

surround [sə'raʊnd]

Sharks **surrounded** the boat.

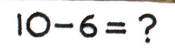

subtract [səb'trækt]

Can you **subtract** six from ten?

study ['stʌdi]

Every night Peter **studies** for his exam.

succeed [sək'si:d]

Peter **succeeded** in passing his exam.

suit [su:t]

This dress doesn't **suit** Aunt Molly. It makes her look fat.

sweat [swɛt]

The runners are **sweating**.

swing [swɪŋ]

The monkey is **swinging** from one bar to another.

switch [swɪtʃ]

The clowns **switched** their hats, making the people laugh.

switch off ['swɪtʃ 'ɒf]

Mother **switched off** the light before leaving the room.

switch on ['swɪtʃ 'ɒn]

Jimmy **switched on** the television.

Tt

teach [tiːtʃ]
Grandmother is **teaching** Kathy how to knit.

thread [θrɛd]
Aunt Molly **threaded** the needle to do some sewing.

tap [tæp]
Linda **tapped** Andy on his shoulder to get his attention.

telephone [ˈtɛlɪfəun]
The house is on fire! **Telephone** the fire brigade.

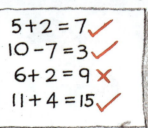

tick [tɪk]
The teacher **ticked** all the sums that were correct.

test [tɛst]
The doctor is **testing** Bobby's eyes to see if he needs glasses.

tidy [ˈtaɪdi]
The desk was a mess so Kathy **tidied** it up.

tick off [ˈtɪk ˈɒf]
Benny **ticked off** the things on the list that he has got for the camp.

throw [θrəu]
Jimmy **threw** the ball to Rusty.

throw away [ˈθrəu əˈweɪ]
The radio was broken so Andy **threw** it **away**.

tie [taɪ]
Scouts learn to **tie** different knots.

tie up ['taɪ 'ʌp]
We are playing cops and robbers.
We are **tying up** the robber so he can't escape.

tighten ['taɪtn]
Willy **tightens** the knot to make sure that the rope will not slip off the tree.

tour [tʊə]
Mandy is **touring** France with a friend.

touch [tʌtʃ]
Bend down and **touch** your toes.

touch down ['tʌtʃ 'daʊn]
Our aeroplane **touched down** at the airport on time.

time [taɪm]
Jimmy is running round the field. Father is **timing** him.

tip [tɪp]
Father **tipped** the waiter for being every helpful.

toast [təʊst]
Linda is **toasting** bread for breakfast.

tip over ['tɪp 'əʊvə]
The bottle **tipped over** and the ketchup spilt on the carpet.

thank [θæŋk]
Jane **thanked** Peter for the birthday present.

tear [tɛə]
Jimmy **tore** his coat on a nail.

tear up [ˈtɛər ˈʌp]
Linda didn't like her drawing, so she **tore** it **up**.

tear out [ˈtɛər ˈaʊt]
Bobby **tore out** a photograph from the newspaper.

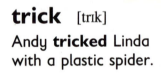

trick [trɪk]
Andy **tricked** Linda with a plastic spider.

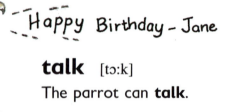

talk [tɔːk]
The parrot can **talk**.

take off [ˈteɪk ˈɒf]
Kathy is **taking off** her coat.

take [teɪk]
Willy is **taking** the cookies from the jar.

take up [ˈteɪk ˈʌp]
Mandy wants to **take up** ballet.

turn [tɜːn]

Mandy is blowing the windmill. See how it **turns**!

turn back ['tɜːn 'bæk]

The path is blocked so Jimmy has to **turn back**.

turn down ['tɜːn 'daʊn]

Father asked Andy to **turn down** the radio because it was too loud.

turn on ['tɜːn 'ɒn]

Mother **turned on** the television to watch the news.

turn off ['tɜːn 'ɒf]

Turn off the bath water before it overflows.

turn up ['tɜːn 'ʌp]

Jimmy **turned up** late for the party.

turn round ['tɜːn 'raʊnd]

The ballet dancer is **turning round** and round.

twinkle ['twɪŋkl]

The stars **twinkle** in the clear sky.

tremble ['trɛmbl]

Andy **trembled** when he saw a monster coming towards him.

train [treɪn]
The trainer is **training** the elephant to stand on its back legs.

trap [træp]
The fox is **trapped** by its tail.

tiptoe ['tɪptəʊ]
The burglar is **tiptoeing** down the hall.

trip [trɪp]
Andy **tripped** over a stone.

treat [tri:t]
Linda **treats** her pet rabbit very well. She feeds it and cleans its cage every day.

travel ['trævl]
Kathy **travels** to school by bus.

trim [trɪm]
Grandfather is **trimming** the hedge.

trace [treɪs]
Andy is **tracing** a picture of a dinosaur.

type [taɪp]
The secretary is **typing** a letter.

tuck [tʌk]
Mother is **tucking** the blanket in around the baby.

Uu

understand [ʌndə'stænd]
Bobby doesn't **understand** why the television won't work.

underline [ʌndə'laɪn]
Kathy is **underlining** all the important words.

unload [ʌn'ləʊd]
The strong men are **unloading** the piano off the truck.

upset [ʌp'sɛt]
The cat **upset** the bowl of fish.

urge [ɜːdʒ]
Jimmy **urged** the dog to jump across the water.

unfasten [ʌn'fɑːsn]
When the car stops you **unfasten** the safety belt.

unlock [ʌn'lɒk]
Father is **unlocking** the door.

untie [ʌn'taɪ]
Untie your shoelaces before you take your shoes off.

undress [ʌn'drɛs]

Kathy got **undressed** ready for her bath.

unpack [ʌn'pæk]

Mandy **unpacks** her suitcase after her trip.

unwrap [ʌn'ræp]

Linda is **unwrapping** her Christmas present.

use [ju:z]

Andy is **using** a blue crayon to colour the car.

unroll [ʌn'rəʊl]

Andy is **unrolling** his painting.

Vv

use up ['ju:z 'ʌp]

The milk is **used up**. We must buy some more.

vacuum ['vækjuəm]

Aunt Molly is **vacuuming** the room.

visit ['vɪzɪt]

We **visited** Grandma at the hospital this afternoon.

vanish ['vænɪʃ]

The magician waved his wand and the rabbit **vanished**.

Ww

wade [weɪd]
Jimmy is **wading** across the water.

wag [wæg]
The puppy is **wagging** its tail happily.

waddle ['wɒdl]
A duck **waddles**.

walk [wɔːk]
Grandfather is **walking** in the park.

wake [weɪk]
Be quiet! Don't **wake** the baby.

walk off with ['wɔːk 'ɒf wɪð]
Andy **walked off with** the first prize in the painting contest.

wake up ['weɪk 'ʌp]
The baby **woke up** because Andy was making a lot of noise.

wait [weɪt]
Bobby is **waiting** at the bus stop for the bus to arrive.

warm [wɔːm]
We are **warming** ourselves round the fire.

wander ['wɒndə]
Simon and Linda are **wandering** through the woods. They are lost.

106

warn [wɔ:n]

The red light **warns** you when the machine gets too hot.

wash [wɒʃ]

Linda **washed** her hands after playing with the clay.

wash up [ˈwɒʃ ˈʌp]

Kathy **washes up** the dishes after dinner.

waste [weɪst]

Turn off the lights so you don't **waste** electricity.

water [ˈwɔ:tə]

Mandy **waters** her plants every day.

weep [wi:p]

Jane is **weeping** over her broken doll.

watch over [ˈwɒtʃ ˈəʊvə]

The mother hen **watches over** her chickens to make sure they are safe.

watch [wɒtʃ]

Bobby is **watching** a game of football on television.

watch out [ˈwɒtʃ ˈaʊt]

You must **watch out** for cars when you cross the road.

wave [weɪv]

Kathy is **waving** goodbye to her friend.

wear [wɛə]
Kathy is **wearing** her mother's shoes.

wear out ['wɛər 'aʊt]
Jimmy's shoes have holes in them. They are **worn out**.

wheel [wi:l]
The nurse is **wheeling** Willy down the corridor.

whip [wɪp]
Linda is **whipping** the cream for the apple pie.

wet [wɛt]
Bobby **wet** his shoes when he stepped into a puddle.

weigh [weɪ]
The butcher is **weighing** the meat.

whisper ['wɪspə]
Whisper the secret so only I can hear you.

whistle ['wɪsl]
Jimmy is **whistling** for his dog.

win [wɪn]
My pet dog **won** first prize at the dog show.

weave [wi:v]
Mandy is **weaving** a basket.

welcome ['wɛlkəm]
Kathy **welcomes** her aunt with flowers.

wind [waɪnd]
The road **winds** around the hill.

wind up [ˈwaɪnd ˈʌp]
Father **winds up** the grandfather clock once a week.

wink [wɪŋk]
Willy **winked** at me.

wish [wɪʃ]
Andy **wished** that he had never gone for a ride with Uncle Roy.

work [wɜːk]
Mr Hart **works** as an engine driver.

wriggle [ˈrɪgl]
The worms **wriggled** around in the jar.

work out [ˈwɜːk ˈaʊt]
The teacher is **working out** the answer to the sum on the blackboard.

wipe [waɪp]
Andy is **wiping** his wet hands on the cloth.

wring [rɪŋ]
Mother is **wringing** the water out of the cloth.

wound [wuːnd]
The soldier was **wounded** in the shoulder.

worry ['wʌri]
Andy is **worried** about his sick grandmother.

wrap [ræp]
Mandy is **wrapping** up the birthday present.

wrinkle ['rɪŋkl]
When Uncle Tom frowns he **wrinkles** his forehead.

wonder ['wʌndə]
Simon can't find his cat. He **wonders** where she is.

write [raɪt]
Linda is **writing** a letter to her cousin.

write down ['raɪt 'daʊn]
Aunt Molly is **writing down** the shopping list so she will not forget what to buy.

Yy

yawn [jɔ:n]
When you are tired you **yawn**.

yell [jɛl]
That baby is **yelling** for his mother.

Zz

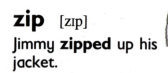

zip [zɪp]
Jimmy **zipped** up his jacket.

zoom [zu:m]
The car **zoomed** past us.